C000257669

MUGHAL EM

A History from Beginning to End

Copyright © 2020 by Hourly History.

Table of Contents

Introduction

Background

The Emergence of Babur

The Rise and Fall of Humayun

The Reign of Akbar the Great

Consolidation and Glory

Art, Architecture and Science in the Mughal Empire

Decline of the Mughal Empire

India Falls under British Control

Legacy

Conclusion

Introduction

For more than 200 years, the Mughal Empire dominated the Indian subcontinent, providing fabulous wealth and unprecedented power for a series of emperors. This empire became the largest economy and manufacturing center in the world, accounting for more than one-quarter of the total GDP on the planet.

The Mughal Empire was defined by trade, especially trade with Europe. Growing demand for products produced and manufactured in India ensured that wealth flowed into the empire and allowed the creation of a vast and efficient infrastructure. Although it was controlled by a sophisticated and complex central administration, the Mughal Empire was generally liberal and pluralist, and it blended the regional cultures of several Indian states with Perso-Islamic and Timurid influence to produce the varied and colorful cultures which define the modern state of India.

However, although it began as a centrally controlled entity, as time progressed, the empire became increasingly influenced by the culture and influence of regions within its boundaries. Towards the end of its period of dominance, the empire was increasingly controlled by powerful regions rather than from the center. This eventually led to its decline and disintegration as well as to the establishment of states and regions which still exist in the Indian subcontinent.

Before the Mughal Empire, the Indian subcontinent was defined by a fragmented patchwork of separate states and cultures. Under this empire and for the first time, the concept of the Indian subcontinent as a single entity began to emerge. Understanding the Mughal Empire is critical to understanding the modern state of India. This is the story of the rise and fall of the mighty Mughal Empire.

Chapter One

Background

"If I were asked under what sky the human mind has most fully developed some of its choicest gifts, has most deeply pondered on the greatest problems of life, and has found solutions, I should point to India."

—Max Muller

The presence of humans in what is now the Indian subcontinent is a relatively recent phenomenon. Archeological evidence suggests that the first people arrived in the Indus River Valley somewhere around 10,000 BCE. These seem to have been mainly small groups of primitive hunter-gatherers, and it wasn't until somewhere around 7,000 BCE that the first evidence of settled human communities emerged, marking the transition from a nomadic way of life to a more pastoral existence revolving around agriculture. Small villages formed and gradually evolved into proto towns, though these were still very primitive.

Then, somewhere around 3,000 BCE, a new culture arose in the Indian subcontinent, one that would dominate for almost 2,000 years but which is still relatively little understood. Up the 1920s, most historians believed that there were two ancient eastern civilizations, Pharaonic Egypt and the Sumerians in the area between the Tigris and

Euphrates Rivers known as Mesopotamia. We know a great deal about these civilizations because they left both written records and vast, monumental structures, some of which still exist today.

In India, it was generally assumed up the end of the nineteenth century that contemporary cultures in the Indian subcontinent were relatively small. Then, in the 1920s, British engineers building a new railway line connecting the cities of Lahore and Karachi in present-day Pakistan began to discover vast numbers of fire-baked mud bricks buried in the dusty earth. This was the first inkling that there might have been a city in the area, and subsequent archeological investigation revealed the existence of a network of mighty cities which had once existed in the plains of present-day Pakistan and India. By the early 1930s, it was becoming clear that the ancient history of India was much more complex and stretched back much further than anyone had previously realized.

These discoveries led to an understanding of what became known as the Indus Valley Civilization (which is sometimes also referred to as the Harappan Civilization or the Sarasvati Civilization), one of the earliest complex, urban human civilizations and a third ancient eastern civilization. The lack of written records means that we know relatively little about this civilization, but we do know that the people of the Indus Valley built very large cities that incorporated, amongst other things, sophisticated systems for drainage and waste disposal. There was also a lively trade system between these people and the various cultures which dominated Mesopotamia during the same period.

Then, in around 1,300 BCE and for reasons we still do not understand, people began to leave the cities of the Indus River Valley. Many reasons have been suggested, including climate change, declining trade with Mesopotamia, and invasion. The lack of records and clear archeological evidence means that we cannot be certain of what happened, but by 1,000 BCE, the cities of the Indus Valley Civilization all lay in ruins and the Indian subcontinent reverted to being controlled by a bewildering number of regional powers, all with their own distinct cultures and languages.

During the period 500-100 BCE, many of these small fiefdoms, the *janapadas*, were consolidated and expanded into larger states, or *mahajanapadas*. For the next 1,500 years, the mahajanapadas grew and waned, each fighting to gain supremacy over the others. None established complete control over the whole subcontinent, though the Gupta, Pala, Rashtrakuta, and Gurjara-Pratihara Empires all became extremely powerful at various times.

During the same period, new religious and ascetic movements which included Jainism and Buddhism gained followers and began to challenge the prominence of the Brahmin priests associated with the traditional Vedic religion. By the end of the fifteenth century, another new religion also emerged in the Punjab called Sikhism, which was based on the teachings of Guru Nanak Dev Ji.

The power of the mahajanapadas was challenged briefly in the fourteenth century by the emergence of a new leader in present-day Uzbekistan. Timur (also known as Timur the Lame and Tamerlane) established a new Mongol Empire with ruthless brutality. Having conquered Persia and much of present-day Russia, he crossed the Indus River and launched an invasion of the Indian subcontinent in 1398. Within months, the armies of Timur had destroyed or conquered many major Indian cities; Delhi was utterly destroyed. By 1405, Timur had conquered Egypt and was planning an invasion of China when he fell ill and died suddenly.

His death was followed by a battle for succession in which no one leader took control of the empire he had created. The capital of the Timurid Empire remained in Samarkand, but the lands it had conquered were left to revert to local control. The defeated mahajanapadas re-established control over the Indian subcontinent and that land reverted to being a fragmented, colorful, and chaotic blend of rulers, cultures, and religions.

However, although no-one realized it at the time, India wasn't quite free of the influence of the all-conquering Timur. In the sixteenth century, one of his descendants would begin the creation of an empire that would finally unite the Indian subcontinent.

Chapter Two

The Emergence of Babur

"India is the cradle of the human race, the birthplace of human speech, the mother of history, the grandmother of legend, and the great grand mother of tradition."

—Mark Twain

The man who would become the founder of the Mughal Empire was not, as you might expect, a member of one of the mahajanapada families. Zahir-ud-din Muhammad was born in the town of Andijan, in the Fergana Valley in present-day Uzbekistan as a member of the Barlas tribe, a group of Mongol extraction. He has become better known to history under the name given to him as a result of his success as a military commander, Babur (meaning "tiger").

His pedigree was certainly notable; he was the eldest son of King Umar Sheikh Mirza, ruler of the Fergana Valley, and he was a direct descendant on his father's side of the great Timur. On his mother's side, he was a direct descendant of another great Mongol leader, Genghis Khan. Given that, perhaps it is no surprise that Babur became one of the most ruthlessly efficient Mongol warlords ever.

Although there were broad rules covering succession in the Mongol tribes, it was by no means certain that a son would succeed his father to the throne. If a man was to become leader, he had to display courage and leadership in battle as well as an ability to unite and command the often feuding Mongol tribes. Babur possessed both qualities in abundance. He first led the Mongols to the city of Samarkand, once the capital of Timur's mighty empire and a place revered by the Mongols. From 1494 to 1512, he led the Mongol armies on a series of attacks on the city and its defenders, forces under the command of Muhammad Shaybani Khan, another descendant of Genghis Khan and ruler of the Uzbeks beyond the Jaxartes River. Twice Babur's armies occupied the city and twice they were thrown out by counterattacks.

Despite this failure and at least two attempts to remove him from power, Babur remained in control. By the early 1520s, he had come to realize that the attempt to retake Samarkand was probably doomed and he faced the power of the Safavid dynasty in Iran if he attempted to expand the area he controlled to the west. Instead, he turned his attention south, towards lands in what is now Afghanistan and beyond, to the Indian subcontinent itself.

During the rule of Timur, Mongol power had extended south into parts of the Punjab, to the area known as Hindustan. This was a wealthy area, rich in natural resources ruled not by a single entity but by a network of bickering mahajanapada families. If Babur could extend his power into this area, he might be able to build the foundations of a new empire.

His armies had occupied Kabul, the capital of Afghanistan in 1504, and in 1522, he seized the strategic city of Kandahar which controlled the route south into India. Between 1522 and 1524, Babur led a number of raids in the Punjab. While these brought plunder, they did not result in his establishing control there. At that time, the Punjab was largely under the control of the Delhi sultanate and the leadership of Sultan Ibrahim Lodi. Part of the problem for Babur was that there was almost constant intrigue against the sultan which made it difficult for him to establish stable alliances in the Punjab.

The fourth and largest raid in the Punjab had to be called off abruptly when Babur was forced to return to deal with an attempted insurrection in Kabul. Then, he was given the opportunity he wanted; Alam Khan, Sultan Ibrahim's uncle, saw a chance to take power for himself and secretly asked Babur for help. In April 1526, Babur met the armies of Sultan Ibrahim at Panipat, 50 miles north of the strategically important city of Delhi. This was the largest and most important battle in which the 32-year-old Mongol leader had been involved.

On paper, the Mongols stood little chance. Babur's army numbered less than 12,000 men. Facing them was an army of more than 100,000 including more than 100 war elephants, one of the most fearsome weapons of the period. However, Babur's troops were seasoned veterans, many mounted, all used to battle and to following their talented leader. Babur also had a new and terrifying weapon: artillery provided by the Ottoman Turks. Babur used the mobility of his cavalry supported by artillery to destroy his enemy, including killing Sultan Ibrahim himself. Within three days, Babur had occupied Delhi. By May 4, he had also occupied the city of Agra, more than 100 miles southwest of Delhi.

At this point, both his followers and those he had conquered seem to have assumed that this was simply another raid and that Babur would soon return to Kabul. What no-one realized was that the Mongol leader had very different plans. His military position was not strong. His army was relatively small and most of his followers were keen to return to their homelands. To the east, Afghan warlords were threatening. To the south, the powerful kingdoms of Malwa and Gujarat were eager to see the Mongol interlopers removed from the subcontinent, and they were supported by Rana Sanga of Mewar, head of a powerful confederacy in Rajasthan.

The Mongol invaders were surrounded by large and powerful military factions who wanted them removed. The prudent course would have been to retreat, but Babur had no intention of leaving Delhi. In March 1527, the small Mongol army faced a much larger army under the command of Rana Sanga. It has been estimated that Rana Sanga led an army of more than 100,000 men supported by over 500 war elephants. Once again, Babur used superior tactics (including using his artillery to cause the war elephants to stampede through their own troops) to achieve a complete victory.

During 1528, Babur led his army into Afghanistan, destroying the power of the warlords who controlled those lands. In May 1529, he led his army to a third victory against a much larger force when he defeated Mahmud Lodi at Ghaghara. This series of victories meant that Babur's position in Delhi was virtually unassailable, but he was given little time to enjoy the respite from battle. In 1530, Babur's eldest son, Humayun, became seriously ill. In response, Babur is said to have pleaded to God to take his life but to spare that of his son. He walked around his son's sickbed seven times to emphasize the solemnity of his vow.

Humayun recovered but Babur almost immediately fell ill. In January 1531, Babur died in the city of Agra at the age of 47. The succession of leadership fell to Humayun. Babur did not create an empire, but his military genius allowed him to create the foundations of what would become one of the most powerful empires on earth. Yet he is not just remembered as a warlord.

Babur was also a gifted Turki poet and a lover of nature; one of his first acts after the conquest of the city of Agra was to build a great garden there. Despite his preoccupation with military matters, he was also a prolific writer; his memoirs, the *Babur-nāmeh*, have become renowned not just because of the ability of the author to describe events in a lively and engaging way but also because of his frequent use of wit and irony.

Chapter Three

The Rise and Fall of Humayun

"Like us many have spoken over this spring, but they were gone in the twinkling of an eye. We conquered the world with bravery and might, but we did not take it with us to the grave."

—Babur

The military victories won by Babur had not created a secure empire; they had simply bought time to allow the consolidation of the territory which had been gained by conquest. The Afghan warlords and the leaders of the mahajanapada families had been defeated in battle, but that did mean that they accepted the existence of Mughal (or Mongol) rule over Delhi and a large part of the subcontinent; they were simply waiting for an opportune moment to oust the invaders.

Nasir-ud-din Muhammad, generally known as Humayun, was just 23 years old when his father died and he inherited the rule of the new Mongol lands in India. His father had already begun to establish the beginnings of an administration that would control Hindustan and had been careful not to antagonize the people of the captured lands by any form of religious intolerance. In retrospect, it is clear that Babur was much more than a warlord; he was also a leader of intelligence and diplomacy who understood that conquered lands cannot be maintained by force alone. He tried to pass these things on to his son, but it is clear that Humayun either failed to understand or deliberately chose to follow another path.

Humayun began his rule with an invasion of the Hindu principality of Kalinjar in Bundelkhand in the present-day Indian state of Madhya Pradesh. This is a mountainous region bisected by steep ravines and barren, rocky plateaus. Humayun's army quickly defeated the army of the local leader but, critically, Humayun moved on to his next conquest without ensuring that the area was fully under Mongol control. This reckless approach was to characterize much of the early period of Humayun's rule. He was adept at winning on the battlefield but less interested in the equally important task of consolidating the areas he had conquered. Humayun was able to take many new lands during the early part of his rule, but this failure meant that many of them reverted to local control as soon as his army had left.

While Humayun was still involved in this unsuccessful invasion of new territory, he was faced with a new threat from the east. A new Afghan warlord, Sher Khan, had established control over many of the Afghan tribes and posed a threat to the Mongol heartlands around Kabul. In 1532, Humayun was forced to turn his attention to this new problem and he became involved in a number of inconclusive battles with the Afghans including an unsuccessful attempt to take the important fortress city of Chunar.

Deciding to temporarily ignore the threat of Sher Khan, Humayun then turned his attention to two provinces in central India: Malwa and Gujarat. Once again he led his armies into these areas and fought successful battles against the local leaders. However, once again he failed to spend the time necessary to ensure that Mongol rule could be permanently established. He then took his army to assist Sultan Mahmud of Bengal who was also involved in fighting the new Afghan leader. For the next few years, Humayun stayed in Gaur, the capital of Bengal, from which he led a number of campaigns against the Afghans, but none were decisive.

In addition this external threat, Humayun also found himself facing a new challenge to his authority from within. His brother Hindal, who he had left in control of Agra and Delhi, began to lose patience with the inability of Humayun to achieve a decisive victory against the Afghans and started to behave more like an independent ruler than a loyal subject of Humayun. Two other brothers, Kamran Mirza and Hindal Mirza, joined Hindal and it was clear that, in order to retain his authority over the Mongol tribes, Humayun urgently needed to defeat Sher Khan, who was now calling himself the shah of Afghanistan.

Finally, in June 1539, Humayun met the forces of Sher Khan in open battle near the village of Chausa, just south of the Ganges River in northeastern India. But, instead of the decisive victory he so badly needed, Humayun was completely defeated. He fled with the remnants of his army to the city of Lahore where he took refuge. Sher Khan followed, and in 1540, Humayun was once again defeated in a large-scale battle. He fled to the Sindh region, but even there he was not safe, and in 1543, he was forced to escape into Iran with just 40 men.

There he pleaded with Safavid Shah Tahmasp to provide assistance in his fight against the Afghans and to help him retake the throne that was now occupied by his brother Hindal. The shah agreed, but on two conditions: Humayun must convert to become a Shi'ite Muslim and he had to agree to the return of Kandahar, an important strategic city and trading center, to the Safavid Empire. With no other options, Humayun agreed, but the shah made no immediate moves to provide an army or support and Humayun became an exile living in Iran. It seemed to most observers that the empire founded by Babur was finished almost before it had begun.

Then, in 1545, Sher Khan died during the siege of the city of Kalinjar and was succeeded by his son Islam Shah. It was soon clear that the new Afghan leader lacked the military and political brilliance of his father. When he died just ten years later, the Afghan confederation split and the tribes became involved in internal warfare. With his Afghan adversaries weakened and with the military support of Shah Tahmasp, Humayun was able to retake the core Mongol cities of Kabul and Kandahar from which he had been usurped by his brother. He then spent considerable time there consolidating his position and ensuring that the leading Mongol families recognized him as their sole leader.

By December 1554, Humayun felt sufficiently secure to lead his armies south, to retake the lands in the Punjab now controlled by his brother. He quickly occupied Lahore and during the first half of 1555, he was able to move cautiously south, capturing first the city of Sirhind and then, in July, taking both Delhi and Agra. After a 12-year absence, Humayun was once again the undisputed leader of the Mongol controlled lands in the Punjab.

Humayun seemed to have learned from his period in exile. Instead of immediately striking out on a new expedition of conquest, he set about consolidating his empire, ensuring that he had the loyalty of the most important families and creating a new administration and infrastructure through which he could rule.

It seemed that the Mughal Empire was back on track when, in January 1556, just six months after re-conquering Delhi, Humayun was descending the steep stairs from the library at his palace in Delhi with his arms full of books when he tripped and fell, striking his head on the stone floor. He died three days later. This was a terrible blow to those who had agreed to support him, and news of his death was kept secret for several weeks while a successor was chosen.

The next ruler of the Mughal was Humayun's 14-year-old son, Abu'l-Fath Jalal-ud-din Muhammad, who was to become known as Akbar the Great.

Chapter Four

The Reign of Akbar the Great

"This great Mughal Emperor was illiterate; he could neither read nor write. However, that had not stopped Akbar from cultivating the acquaintance of the most learned and cultured poets, authors, musicians, and architects of the time—relying solely on his remarkable memory during conversations with them."

—Indu Sundaresan

Akbar inherited a fragile empire and because of his youth, rule initially passed to a regent, Bairam Khan, until the new leader came of age. However, the new emperor quickly showed a strong personality and was always involved in decision-making. Under the rule of the new leader, the Mughal Empire would emerge as the most powerful military, social, and political grouping in the Indian subcontinent.

From the very beginning, Akbar was keen on innovation and reform. The Mughal army had always used firearms, but under the rule of Akbar, it became one of the world's leading exponents of this new weapon technology. New artillery was obtained from the Ottoman Empire and gunpowder experts from as far away as Portugal were brought in to improve the ability of the army to use these weapons. And it wasn't just cannons that gave the Mughal army an advantage; under Akbar's rule and due in part to his personal interest, matchlock muskets were distributed to large numbers of Mughal soldiers. This became so prevalent that for a time, this empire was referred to as the "Gunpowder Empire." The technical advantage that this gave the Mughals over every other contemporary army on the subcontinent may help to explain why it was so successful during the period of Akbar's rule.

One of the first challenges to Mughal rule during the reign of Akbar came from Hemu, a former minister and general for one of the Sur rulers, who had proclaimed himself Hindu emperor and established control over part of the Indo-Gangetic plains formerly ruled by the Mughals. Akbar's first test as a military leader came in a quick defeat of Hemu before he was forced to confront Sikander Shah Suri who had established a power base in the Punjab which threatened Mughal lands.

In a year of fighting, Akbar was able to defeat Shah Suri and establish Mughal control over the city of Ajmer, the main route to Rajputana, the fertile and wealthy lands of central India. In 1560, Akbar led a Mughal army south into Rajputana and quickly conquered the provinces of Malwa and Garha, a barren and thinly populated area which was of interest to the Mughals mainly because it contained large herds of elephants that would become part of the Mughal army.

By 1576, the Mughal armies had conquered all of Rajputana, and soon after, they began the annexation of areas of western and eastern India. By 1585, Akbar was leading his troops south once again, capturing the city of Kashmir in the Upper Indus River valley. Under Akbar's leadership, the area controlled by the Mughal Empire more than tripled in size. The main difference between Akbar and his father and grandfather was that he quickly made it clear that these weren't simply raids; his intention was to ensure than the new lands were completely subjugated and integrated into the growing empire.

While Akbar's military leadership was clearly very competent, it is in the control and administration of the new lands that he made the greatest contribution to the establishment of a secure base for the empire. He increased trade with European nations, and the empire quickly developed a strong and stable economy which in turn led to sustained commercial expansion and continued economic development. This allowed Akbar to create a new system of taxation, the *dahsala* system, to ensure a steady flow of income to support the war effort. The system required people in areas controlled by the Mughals to pay taxes at a rate calculated as one-third of the average value of produce over the previous ten years, to be paid annually in cash. The new system also took account of periods of drought or shortage during which remission was given to taxpayers. This system was not popular, but it was generally seen as more fair than the previous sectarian system which taxed non-Muslims more and it ensured the flow of cash that the empire needed.

Akbar introduced a centralized administration which ensured that his policies were carried out throughout the lands controlled by the empire. He also instituted a policy of integrating conquered lands into the empire by deft political maneuvering and the marriage of members of his family to the ruling families of the conquered areas.

In addition, Akbar oversaw sweeping reforms that affected almost every aspect of life under Mughal rule. For example, under his leadership, the Mughal Empire became a secular state, an essential move in lands so religiously, socially, and culturally diverse. Although most of its leaders remained Muslim, Akbar understood that to discriminate against the many Hindus and other religions within the empire would simply encourage dissent. He even decreed that Hindus who had been forced to convert to the Muslin religion under previous Mughal rulers were to be permitted to re-convert if they chose. Under his enlightened rule, the Mughal Empire was transformed into one that was recognized as liberal, pluralist, and encouraging cultural and social integration. It was this as much as his military conquests that established the true beginning of the Mughal Empire.

Akbar's court also became a center of learning and the arts. He encouraged debates between different Muslim sects and other religions. He established a number of libraries, including the great library of Fatehpur Sikri which was exclusively reserved for use by women, something that was unheard of at the time. The Persian influence which Akbar brought to India (his mother was a Persian princess) gradually melded with indigenous culture to create something entirely new: an Indo-Persian culture which would dominate the Mughal Empire.

When Akbar died in 1605 at the age of 63 following a bout of dysentery, he had ruled the Mughal Empire for 50 years. In that time, he developed his empire from a temporary focus of Mongol raids into a permanent and powerful feature of the Indian subcontinent with its own distinct culture. Although the contributions of Babur and Humayun were significant, it was the third emperor, Akbar, who truly created the Mughal Empire.

Akbar was succeeded by his son, Nur-ud-din Muhammad Salim, known as Jahangir. However, the new emperor would prove to be much less adept than his father.

Chapter Five

Consolidation and Glory

"The city palace is a complex of courtyards, gardens and buildings right in the center of the old city, enlarged and adopted over centuries."

—Lindsay Brown and Amelia Thomas

Almost as soon as Jahangir ascended the throne in late 1605, he faced a challenge from an unexpected source; his own eldest son, Prince Khusrau Mirza, claimed to be the rightful heir to the throne and instigated a revolt against his father. This rebellion was quickly crushed, and Khusrau Mirza was eventually killed by Jahangir's third son, Prince Khurram.

Khurram became Jahangir's favorite, and in 1622, the prince was sent to fight an uprising in Mughal lands and he easily defeated the forces of the cities of Ahmednagar, Bijapur, and Golconda in western India. However, after his victories, Prince Khurram also led his armies in a rebellion against his father. This was defeated and Khurram was imprisoned in Agra.

Part of the reason for revolts led by two of his sons was the fact that Jahangir was seen by many people as a weak and inefficient leader and some wanted to see him replaced with someone stronger. Jahangir had inherited a strong empire and a thriving economy, and he seemed content to enjoy the life of an emperor without being too concerned with the running of the empire. Later accounts claim that he frequently withdrew from public life for extended periods, and this became associated with a supposed addiction to opium and the daily consumption of prodigious amounts of wine.

What Jahangir did have was a fascination with art and architecture. He amassed a vast collection of art and became the patron of a number of prominent artists, encouraging them to experiment with new styles. One recent historian compared Jahangir to the dissolute Roman Emperor Nero and said of him that had he "been head of a Natural History Museum, he would have been a better and happier man."

In 1627, after 21 years of rule, Jahangir became ill and quickly died. The succession of Mughal emperors was not only based on primogeniture, but there was also an assessment of who might make the strongest emperor. Although Prince Khurram was still in disgrace after the rebellion against his father, he was thought likely to make the most formidable emperor, and in January 1628, he was placed on the Mughal throne as Shah Jahan.

Almost immediately, he confirmed just how determined he was by ordering a round of executions of anyone who might also have a legitimate claim to the throne including his brother Shahryar, his nephews Dawar and Garshasp and his cousins Tahmuras and Hoshang. Brutal and arbitrary though they may have been, these executions ensured that there would be no effective challenge to the rule of the new emperor.

The army of the Moghul Empire expanded to its greatest extent during the rule of Shah Jahan, reaching a total size of almost one million men at arms, making it by far the most powerful military force in the Indian subcontinent and one of the largest in the world. The army began to dominate the empire during the reign of Shah Jahan; the nobility, the main source of officers in the army, increased by over four times during this period, and senior officers in the army became extremely powerful even during times of peace.

The army was used relatively little for conquest or expansion in this period, being used instead as a means of ensuring the docility of the people ruled in the Mughal lands. Rebellions by the Bundela Rajputs and by Sikhs in Lahore were quickly and effectively crushed. The only territorial expansion of the empire occurred when Shah Jahan ordered the annexation of three Rajput kingdoms of Baglana, Mewar, and Bundelkhand.

Shah Jahan also found himself dealing for the first time with European settlers, and these also caused some problems. The Portuguese established a settlement at Port Hooghly-Chinsurah in western Bengal, and the aggressive proselytizing of their Jesuit priests so infuriated the emperor that he ordered them expelled.

However, not all Shah Jahan's time was spent on military and political matters; he, like his father, was fascinated by architecture and he became one of the most prominent patrons of architecture in the empire. When his favorite wife, Mumtaz Mahal, died in June 1631, the emperor called upon architects from all over India and from as far as Europe to collaborate on the design of a grand mausoleum in her memory. The building was completed in 1643 and cost a staggering sum, approximately equivalent to $900 million today. It has become one of the most iconic buildings in the world and better known by the name later given to it—the Taj Mahal.

Expenditure in general was beginning to be a problem during the reign of Shah Jahan. The income needed to support the massive standing army was almost more than the revenue coming in from taxation, and when this was combined with the emperor's lavish spending on artistic and architectural projects, it was clear that an unsustainable situation was developing.

When Shah Jahan became ill in 1658, this immediately prompted a fight for the succession amongst his sons. Three immediately raised armies and began a brief but bitter civil war. The eventual victor was his third son, Muhi-ud-Din Muhammad, known as Aurangzeb. He defeated the other claimants to the throne just as his father staged an unexpected recovery. Undaunted, Aurangzeb had his father declared incompetent and confined him to a fortress in Agra. All of his brothers were killed or executed in the civil war, and Aurangzeb became the sixth Mughal emperor in the summer of 1658.

Under his rule, the Mughal Empire would expand even more to become a world superpower. Some expansion was achieved by the use of direct military occupation, but a great deal was achieved by sheer intimidation; no-one could stand up to the might of the Mughal army, and when the emperor suggested that large parts of southern India might perhaps choose to join his empire, there was little active dissent.

The sheer numbers are daunting. Under the rule of Aurangzeb, the area of the Mughal Empire expanded to cover more than four million square kilometers and included over one hundred and fifty million subjects. Imperial revenue was more than ten times that of France, at that time the wealthiest of the European nations. The economy of the Mughal Empire exceeded even that of the contemporary Qing Dynasty China, and the empire became the largest source of manufacture in the world with a GDP exceeding that of all the European powers combined.

For all the power and wealth that his rule brought, Aurangzeb is chiefly remembered as a pious and frugal leader. He was said to have memorized the complete Koran, and under his rule, expenditure on the ostentatious art and architecture which had so beguiled his predecessors dwindled almost to nothing. His piety also led to the abandonment of the policy of liberalism which had previously characterized the empire, and he introduced new taxes which specifically targeted non-Muslims. Some Hindu temples were demolished, and activities such as music, gambling, fornication outside marriage, and the consumption of alcohol and narcotics were prohibited and transgressions severely punished.

Late in his rule, the Mughal Empire was threatened by a revolt amongst the Pashtun tribes in the north of the empire. The revolt spread and, despite the personal intervention of Aurangzeb who led his armies, Mughal power in the north was severely reduced. Although the emperor was able to regain control of the main trade routes in the area, this area was never effectively brought back under full control.

The last 20 years of Aurangzeb's reign were spent seeking further expansion of the empire through fighting the Marathas, a confederation of Jats, Sikhs, and Afghan tribes in the Deccan Plateau in western and southern India. This was a war of insurgency where the Marathas refused to meet the massive Mughal army in open battle. From 1697 to 1707, it has been estimated that the Mughals lost an average of 100,000 men each year in an unsuccessful attempt to take this inhospitable land. The emperor remained personally involved, and in early 1707, the 88-year-old emperor became ill and died at his battle-camp in Bhingar near Ahmednagar.

Despite the expense and casualties inflicted by the war with the Marathas, Aurangzeb's empire was still the most powerful military and political force on the planet at the time of his death. No-one could have guessed that, within little more than 40 years of his death, the Mughal Empire would be reduced to a shadow of its former glory.

Chapter Six

Art, Architecture and Science in the Mughal Empire

"The Taj Mahal rises above the banks of the river like a solitary tear suspended on the cheek of time."

—Rabindranath Tagore

Art and architecture both flourished in the Mughal Empire and especially in the period from 1556 to 1707. Humayun's forced exile in Persia exposed him to the intricate and ornate art of the Safavid Empire, and he returned with an appreciation for that style and with a Persian wife. From that time on, the stylistic influences on Mughal art were a unique fusion of Timurid, Indian, and Persian, which created something new and distinctive.

Humayun's early and unexpected death gave him little time to appreciate these things after he was able to restore the fragmented empire but his son, Akbar, was able to devote some of his considerable energy to the creation of breathtaking public architecture. Humayun's tomb, commissioned by Akbar's wife Hamida Banu Begum in 1652, is one of the best-known examples of the architecture which emerged under Akbar.

This was the first garden tomb in the Indian subcontinent and was designed by a Persian architect. It was constructed almost entirely of red sandstone (the first large building to use this expensive building material) topped by a dome of polished white marble. The overall design is recognizably Islamic, but this is melded with indigenous Rajasthani decorative elements including ornate inlaid patterns created from small pieces of stone. This fusion of Persian and Indian styles became a feature of virtually all the large architecture projects overseen during the long reign of Akbar.

One of the most notable projects was the construction of Akbar's royal city, Fatehpur Sikri, which included a mosque of unusual design, featuring a prayer hall with a shallow dome and a vast central courtyard accessed through the Buland Darwaza, the largest gateway in India at the time of its construction.

By the time of Akbar's death in 1605, the fusion of style elements with origins including Persian, Turkic, Timurid Iranian, Central Asian as well as Indian Hindu and Muslim had produced a rich, ornate, and opulent new look which was continued by Jahangir whose contributions included the tomb of Itmad-ud-Daula and the great mosque at Lahore.

Yet it was under the next Mughal emperor, Shah Jahan, that the best-known expressions of Mughal architecture were produced. Buildings of complex design, richly decorated with inlays and patterns of bewildering complexity, these are embodiments of the wealth and power of the now vast empire. The Taj Mahal remains the best-known creation from this period, but the Jama Masjid in Delhi, the Moti Masjid in Agra Fort, and the Sheesh Mahal in Lahore Fort are equally striking and beautiful.

It is unsurprising that during the reign of the austere and pious Aurangzeb, there was less focus on the creation of ornate and expensive public buildings though the Badshahi mosque is attributed to him and includes novel construction featuring bricks faced with red sandstone. After Aurangzeb, the declining fortunes of the Mughal Empire left little spare income or resources for the creation of vast public buildings. The creation of the Taj Mahal, for example, was said to have involved 20,000 men working over a period of 12 years. While this type of massive project was possible during the heyday of the empire, it was not feasible after the death of Aurangzeb when all resources were needed to ensure the very survival of the empire. Mughal architecture did not end after the death of Aurangzeb, but it produced little that was striking or new.

Moghul art followed a similar pattern. The ornate and colorful style which emerged during Humayun's rule was continued throughout the reigns of Akbar, Jahangir, and Shah Jahan with stunning illustrations of the natural world as well as advances in portraiture and narrative painting (Jahangir was particularly fond of paintings which illustrated events from his own life). Then, as with architecture, under the reign of Aurangzeb, the production of new works of art declined, and the artists who formed the Mughal academy disbanded and went to work instead mainly for Rajput royal families.

Just like the empire itself, the art and architecture of the Mughal Empire represent a blend of styles and influences from a number of religious, social, and cultural backgrounds, and its rich designs echo the wealth of the empire at its height. This produced an instantly recognizable and ornate style which was copied by many later architects and artists.

Science also flourished under the early Moghul Empire, and it too benefitted from a melding of knowledge. We have already discussed the importance of gunpowder and firearm technology to the armies of the empire, and Mughal scientists and technicians became amongst the most knowledgeable in the world about this emerging technology; by 1657, Mughal armies were using not just firearms but advanced weapons such as grenades and rockets.

Mughal science also made notable advances in less warlike directions. For example, a combination of advanced Islamic celestial observational techniques and instruments and new Indian computational developments led to the emergence of more accurate and more advanced astronomical observation. Mughal astronomers understood more about the night sky than any who had come before.

Mughal metalworkers were amongst the most advanced in the world, and Damascus steel produced the sharpest and most durable blades in the world at the time. In irrigation too, Mughal engineers and scientists made notable advances. Agricultural land was made more productive by the use of complex irrigation systems, and many cities ruled by the Mughals benefitted from the introduction of elaborate public water supplies. Akbar, for example, had an enormous dam built, which fed a system of public fountains and an artificial lake in the center of Fatehpur Sikri. Shah Jahan created a number of canals which allowed both transport and the distribution of water to parts of the empire. During his reign, Agra became known as "the waterfront city."

Chapter Seven

Decline of the Mughal Empire

"I have sinned terribly, and I do not know what punishment awaits me."

—Aurangzeb

Although the Mughal Empire still looked formidable at the time of Aurangzeb's death in 1707, the reality was very different. That emperor's obsession with crushing the Marathas led to a war that lasted more than 20 years and drained the resources of the mighty Mughal Empire. His absence from the capital for much of this time also undermined the authority of the emperor and left subordinates to squabble over power. Aurangzeb's rejection of the relatively liberal policies of his predecessors also contributed to the fragmentation of the empire. Hindus in particular, who formed a sizeable portion of the population, had enjoyed fair and equable treatment while the Mughal Empire was a secular state. With Aurangzeb's emphasis on creating a Muslim state, Hindus became discriminated against, especially in the form of the *jizyah*, taxes which were levied only on non-Muslims.

Aurangzeb died without appointing a successor, and his sons went to war over control of the Mughal throne. The victor was Muhammad Mu'azzam who was crowned as Bahadur Shah in June 1707. The new emperor inherited a vast and sprawling empire which was already facing opposition for the outside as well as increasing internal unrest. He immediately began to address this, repealing many of the religious edicts instituted by his father. The *jizyah* was never formally repealed, but under the reign of Bahadur Shah, it was quietly abandoned.

Given time, this more moderate new emperor might have been able to restore the flagging fortunes of the empire, but instead, he died suddenly in Lahore in February 1712 after ruling for less than five years. Much of his rule had been occupied with the suppression of various rebellions, and his sudden death plunged the Mughal Empire into a period of terminal instability.

Bahadur Shah's death was followed by a period of seven years in which competing factions fought for the throne. In 1719 alone, four new emperors took the throne and were quickly displaced. Finally, in 1719, Muhammad Shah, the grandson of Bahadur Shah, became emperor and he would rule for almost 30 years. However, he presided mainly over the break-up of the empire. The extended period of chaos from 1712 to 1719 had allowed the Mughal Empire's rivals to extend their power. The Marathas occupied vast tracts of central India which had previously been controlled by the empire. Sikhs in the Punjab allied themselves with the Marathas and took control of a vast swathe of formerly Mughal territory around the city of Ajmer. The rise of a new and powerful Iranian leader, Nadir Shah, led to an invasion of Mughal territory and eventually to the occupation and sack of Delhi itself.

Loss of territory led to a loss of revenue, and the once invincible Mughal army declined both in size and power. Once, more than a million men had served in the Mughal army, but by 1739, it could muster no more than 200,000 men spread over a still large territory. Yet the greatest threat to the empire came not from external enemies but from a growing feeling that the empire was no longer viable, which in turn encouraged many of the territories it controlled to look to independence.

The new emperor attempted to use diplomacy and guile to counter the new threats. For example, the Mughal army was simply not strong enough to resist the Persian invasion led by Nadir Shah which began in May 1738. The Mughals were forced to give up large tracts of land west of the Indus River to the Persian invaders. In response, Muhammad Shah could only hope for assistance from the arch-rivals of the Persians, the powerful Ottoman Empire.

He did gain some support for the Ottoman Empire, but not as he hoped, direct military intervention against Nadir Shah. The Mughal Empire was forced to cede a great deal of productive and important land to the Persians. Then, in 1747, Nadir Shah was assassinated and a new Persian leader took charge, Ahmad Shah Durrani. Almost immediately, Durrani began an invasion intended to take the Peshwar province from the weakened Mughal Empire. Losing Peshwar would almost certainly have led to the complete disintegration of the empire, and Muhammad Shah was forced to respond. This invasion culminated in the Battle of Manupur in early 1748 where the Mughal army met the Persian armies of Durrani. The outcome was a victory for the Mughal army, and this is generally recognized as the last major Mughal victory and the last desperate effort of a rapidly fragmenting empire.

Although it was an important victory, the scale of casualties on the Mughal side at Manupur was so great that the emperor understood that he would be unable to resist continuing rebellions from Sikhs and Marathas. When he heard of the scale of losses, Muhammad Shah retired to his private apartments and refused to leave. He died on April 16, 1748. The official cause was given as "grief."

The death of Muhammad Shah did not mark the formal end of the Mughal Empire, but after this time internal and external challenges led to increasing fragmentation and a loss of power and authority. By the time that the sixteenth emperor, Shah Alam II, came to the throne in 1760, there was a popular saying in Persia that "The empire of Shah Alam stretches from Delhi to Palam." Palam is a suburb of Delhi. Soon even control of Delhi was beyond reach. An afghan invasion in 1760 took control of the city and the emperor was only able to return by accepting the protection and military support of the Marathas.

Chapter Eight

India Falls under British Control

"The East India Company's domination of the Indian economy was based on its private army."

—Robert Trout

The protection of the Mughal Empire by the Marathas enabled Shah Alam to continue to reign, but his power was severely reduced. However, the final destruction of the empire was brought about not by another great power seeking to extend its influence but by a commercial company seeking profit for its shareholders.

The Portuguese and the French were the first European powers to establish a presence in the Indian subcontinent, but in 1634, a British trading company, the East India Company, had been granted permission by the Mughal Emperor Jahangir to establish a small British trading post in Bengal. This company had originally been formed in 1600 to establish trade routes between Britain and the East Indies, but by the dawn of the eighteenth century, it had become extremely powerful, operating its own warships to protect merchant vessels.

By the mid-1700s, India had become an important trade partner for Britain and a significant source of profits for the

East India Company. In addition to warships, the company took advantage of the increasing weakness of the Mughal Empire by creating its own army of mercenary soldiers, mainly comprising Indian sepoys commanded by British officers. By 1778, this army had reached a size of almost 70,000 well-trained, well-equipped men, making it one of the most formidable military forces on the subcontinent. This private army was so successful that the East India Company soon controlled most of Bengal.

In 1775, the army of the East India Company went to war with the Marathas. The outcome of this war was not decisive (the British would fight two more wars against the Marathas before finally defeating them), but it severely reduced the power and authority of the Marathas.

In October 1764, the East India Company met the Mughal Empire in battle near Buxar, a small town on the banks of the Ganga river. The army of the East India Company was relatively small, numbering less than 7,000 soldiers, and it faced not just what remained of the Mughal army under the command of Emperor Shah Alam II but also contingents supplied by the Nawabs of Bengal and Awadh Shuja-ud-Daula. The Indian force numbered more than 40,000 men in total.

The outcome was a decisive victory for the East India Company. The British suffered around 600 casualties while inflicting more than 6,000 on their enemies. Following this military catastrophe, Emperor Shah Alam II was forced to align himself with the British, and soon the East India Company replaced the Marathas as the main protectors of what remained of the Mughal Empire.

By 1857, the empire was little more than a paper entity, with the East India Company effectively ruling its territory. Then, in that year, there was a large-scale and organized rebellion against British rule in India. The rebellion began in Meerut and the rebels soon controlled large areas of the northwestern provinces of India. The rebels arrived in Delhi where they declared the 81-year-old Mughal emperor, Bahadur Shah Zafar, to be the emperor of India.

The East India Company reacted quickly and brutally. Their army moved against the rebels and massacred anyone thought to have been involved. It has been estimated that more than 800,000 people died as a result, many of whom were civilians. By June 1858, the rebellion had been crushed. Because he had been seen to support the rebels, Emperor Bahadur Shah Zafar was tried, deposed, and sent into exile in Rangoon in Burma. His exile is generally taken to formally mark the end of the Mughal Empire, though the truth is that its declining power meant that it had not been a major factor in the Indian subcontinent for a century. Emperor Bahadur Shah Zafar died in November 1862 while still in exile in Rangoon.

In the same year, the British government formally took over control of lands in India held by the East India Company. The British Raj was thus created, and in 1876, Queen Victoria formally assumed the title of Empress of India.

Chapter Nine

Legacy

"Artists are the delight of the world."

—Humayun

The Indian subcontinent was and is a place of rich cultural, social, and religious diversity. This diversity made it difficult for any one group to establish widespread control until the secular, enlightened, and liberal attitudes of early Mughal emperors enabled them not just to conquer vast tracts of land but to assimilate the people of those lands into the empire. No subsequent group which sought to control India could ignore this approach and the promotion of largely peaceful diversity became the hallmark of most of the rulers who followed.

It is the artistic and architectural achievements of the Mughals which remain most visible today. The colorful, ornate, stylized form of art which is today recognized as typically "Indian" actually has its origins in the melding of cultures of the Mughal Empire. Some of the architecture created during this time has become not just famous as a tourist attraction but, as in the case of the Taj Mahal for example, a visual icon that has come to represent the very essence of India.

Even language in India owes some of its origins to the Mughal Empire. During the rule of the early emperors,

Persian was the official language of the royal court and of the administration of the empire. During the rule of Aurangzeb, this began to change. The common language used in Delhi came to be referred to as *Zaban-e-Urdu*, which seems to mean "language of the army camp." This language spread across the Mughal Empire and today, over 60 million people speak Urdu which is also the official national language of Pakistan and one of the languages officially recognized in India.

Even some of the curries which are India's best-known cuisine began in the Mughal Empire. Like every other aspect of the empire, this cuisine came from a melding of the cooking styles and ingredients of Persia and the Timurid lands with the regional cuisines of northern India. If you have ever eaten a biriyani, korma, rogan josh, chicken tikka, or tandoori chicken, you have eaten food which originated in the Mughal Empire.

The influence of Mughal cuisine can still be seen in regional dishes in present-day India, Bangladesh, and Pakistan, and its cooking style is used in traditional northern Indian cuisines, particularly in Delhi and Uttar Pradesh, as well as in the southern Indian city of Hyderabad in Telangana.

However, one of the greatest legacies left behind by this empire is that which relates to education. Emperor Akbar introduced widespread education centers across the empire and opened schools and vocational colleges which were open to all citizens regardless of religious or cultural affiliation and provided education without fees. This policy of free, universal education for all was continued by Jahangir and Shah Jahan, though under Aurangzeb, many

Hindu schools and colleges were closed and there was some attempt to restrict education to Muslims only.

The era of the Mughal Empire has also provided a rich history from which a great deal of contemporary entertainment has been provided in India. One of the very first Bollywood blockbusters, *Mughal-e-Azam* (1960), was a love story set in the Mughal Empire. Another early Bollywood smash hit, *Taj Mahal* (1963), tells the fictionalized musical story of the love affair between Shah Jahan and his wife, Mumtaz Mahal. Even more recent offerings such as *Jodhaa Akbar* (2008) is based loosely on the life of Emperor Akbar and his love for a Rajput princess, Jodha.

The Mughal Empire has also provided inspiration for a number of popular novels, including *The Crows of Agra* by Sharath Komarraju, which is set during the early years of the life of Akbar, and *The Twentieth Wife* by Indu Sundaresan which is set later during the reign of Akbar.

These movies and novels are heavily fictionalized treatments of life in the Mughal Empire, but their continuing popularity illustrates the extent to which the turbulent history of this multi-cultural empire has become embedded in modern Indian culture. As Indian writer and author of the *Taj Trilogy* Indu Sundaresan notes, "There is little about the Mughals that's not fascinating. They lived larger-than-life lives, they loved passionately; they built palaces, forts, monuments fervently; they came to India to conquer and stayed on to leave an indelible mark on India's history."

The Mughals may have arrived as invaders, but they rapidly assimilated and became assimilated by the culture and values of northern India. From that arose a vibrant, colorful multi-cultural empire which formed the basis for much of what can be seen in present-day India and Pakistan.

The Mughal Empire changed the Indian subcontinent completely. It brought an influx of ideas, culture, and cuisine from other parts of the world and through interaction with indigenous people, these were blended into something completely new. So much and so many things that are now thought to be "typically Indian" actually originated with this Mongol invasion.

Conclusion

The rise to prominence of the Mughal Empire was astonishingly rapid. When Humayun returned from exile in Persia in 1555, he ruled over a relatively small area that was far from settled. Less than one hundred years later, Shah Jahan ruled over the largest and most powerful empire in the world and controlled the strongest economy and manufacturing base and the largest army in the Indian subcontinent.

However, the decline and fall of the empire were equally rapid. Move forward another hundred years and the empire was fragmented and existed in name only. In retrospect, the reasons are easy to see. The empire had become so physically large that effective administration was virtually impossible. Maintaining the vast army required to secure the empire against internal unrest and to protect its borders became so expensive that it was finally beyond even the staggering wealth of the empire.

Perhaps the element which contributed most to the decline of the empire was the long rule of the sixth emperor, Aurangzeb. Although in many ways he was an intelligent and restrained ruler, Aurangzeb undid the policy of tolerance and inclusion which his predecessors had instituted. Aurangzeb's obsession with defeating the Marathas and the vast expense of his 20-year campaign also left his successors ruling a relatively impoverished and increasingly fragmented empire.

Despite its relatively short period of absolute control, the Mughal Empire left a legacy which has helped to define present-day India and Pakistan. The vibrant, multi-cultural culture first engendered by the Mughal Empire is still evident today and the art, architecture, and cuisine of the empire have become for many people iconic representations of the subcontinent.

The legacy of the Mughal Empire endures today and will continue to influence life for millions of people for the foreseeable future.

Printed in Great Britain
by Amazon

31873314R00030